I0166056

C. W. King

Talismans and amulets

C. W. King

Talismans and amulets

ISBN/EAN: 9783742830166

Manufactured in Europe, USA, Canada, Australia, Japa

Cover: Foto ©ninafisch / pixelio.de

Manufactured and distributed by brebook publishing software
(www.brebook.com)

C. W. King

Talismans and amulets

By CHARLES W. KING, M.A.

ALTHOUGH these terms are usually confounded together, their proper meaning is entirely distinct. *Talisman* is no more than the corruption in the Arabian mouth of the Greek ἀποτέλεσμα the influence of a planet or Zodiacal sign upon the person born under the same ; whence came the technical term for astrology ἡ ἀποτελεσματική. Now the influence of every *degree* in each sign was typified by a fanciful figure, or group, painted in the " Table of Myriogeneses " (a term to be explained farther on), and thus, by a natural transition, in course of time the symbol itself usurped the name, *Apotelesma*, of the idea which at first it was only meant to portray. A *talisman* was therefore by its very nature a *sigil*, symbolical figure, whether engraved in stone or metal, or drawn upon parchment and paper. An excellent illustrative example is the one figured by Raspe, No. 354, where the Abraxas god, carrying the lustral vase, is encircled by the ungrammatical invocation of its Alexandrian fabricator, ΠΡΟΣ ΠΑΝΤΑΣ ΑΝΘΡΩΠΟΝ ΔΟΤΑΙ ΧΑΡΙΝ ΤΟΙΣ ΦΕΡΟΥΣΙΝ " Give unto the bearers favour in the sight of all men." The talisman, therefore, served both to procure love and to avert danger from its possessor.

The latter purpose alone was the object of the *amulet*, a word probably derived, to judge by the thing it originally designated, from rustic Latinity, its root being *amolior*, " to do away with," or baffle. The, at first sight, so specious etymology from the Arabic *hamalet*, " suspended," is overthrown by Pliny's notice of its primary signification, which shows it to be a genuine old Latin term, and not imported by the Oriental magicians of imperial times. For he cites the word as the countryfolks' name for the cyclamen, " which ought to be planted in every house, if it be indeed true that where it is grown poisonous drugs have no power to harm ;

on which account they call the flower *amuletum.*" [1]   Afterwards the name of the flower came to be applied to other natural objects possessing the like virtue ; for Pliny, speaking of amber, observes "infantibus alligari amuleti modo prodest." It may here be remarked that the only *amuletum* provided by nature that preserves its ancient reputation in our own day is the "child's caul," still to be seen advertised at the regular price of five guineas, and readily saleable to sea-faring folks as a sure protection from all danger of drowning. But with the Romans, as Lampridius tells us (Diadumenian. III.), its efficacy was of a different kind, and in fact only affected that profession held of all others in the greatest detestation by sailors ; for the Roman midwives used to sell the membrane stripped off the fortunate infant's head "to credulous lawyers, who believed that they prospered through possessing it."

Many other things, both animal and vegetable, the stranger in shape the more efficacious, had the power of counteracting the ever-dreaded Evil Eye ; amongst which stands pre-eminent the Greek *phallus,* the Latin *fascinum,* either represented in its actual form or by the fist with the fingers so closed as to suggest the same obscene idea. The first stroke only of the fearful influence was fatal, hence whatever diverted it from the person, in so doing destroyed its force. For such a purpose what could serve better than anything odd, strange, indecent, and thereby unlikely to be exposed to view ? The *phallus* was, of course, the first to suggest itself, and was followed, more decorously, by numerous other articles bearing some supposed analogy to the idea it conveyed. With this meaning a locust, or rather mole-cricket, of bronze was set up by Pisistratus, says Hesychius, in the Acropolis as a καταχήνη (literally "a thing to stare at"), or charm against the Evil Eye ; [2] and the insect itself is perpetually repeated on gems with a similar intention. The skull of an ass stuck upon a pole in the middle of a vineyard was accounted the best preservative against blight ; and this usage long held its ground in Tuscany, for Boccaccio makes an amusing use

---

[1] "A nostris Tuber Terræ vocatur, in omnibus serenda domibus si verum est ubi sata est nihil nocere mala medicamenta : *amuletum* vocant : narrantque et ebrietatem representari addita in vinum."

[2] With the same view "certain laughable objects" were set up in front of potters' furnaces, to avert the mischances to which their manufacture is so peculiarly liable. Pollax.

of it in one of his tales, where the lady telegraphs there-with her husband's absence to her lover, by turning the skull in a particular direction. (Day vi. Nov. 1.)

I shall now proceed to illustrate the foregoing definitions by describing the most remarkable examples in either class that have come under my observation. Those only are quoted which declare their intention in an intelligible language, to the exclusion of the purely Gnostic, although, by the light of the former, we may safely conjecture the purport of those long inscriptions in an unknown tongue, which, if interpreted, may be supposed to contain prayers of the same kind as others less carefully shrouded from the understanding of the profane.

A large round disk of loadstone, still extremely powerful (belonging to myself) is engraved with the three Graces, and the legend—ZHCEC ZABATI—' long life to thee, Sabatius !' Reverse, Horus seated on the lotus, with ANA-ΘANABΛΛ in a continuous circle around him : on the margin, declaring the purpose of the talisman, CY NIKAC ΠANTEC (sic). Of much the same character is another gem of mine, a bloodstone bearing a spirited engraving of a race-horse carrying the palm of victory in his mouth, and his name, TIBERIS, added. The reverse exhibits the Power to whose favour the pious *turfite* of old had ascribed his success, in the person of the Abraxas god with the invocation on the stone's edge, ZACTA IAW BAPIA.* Raspe's invaluable reper-tory[3] supplies many curious instances of the sort. His No. 630, a magic symbol inscribed with the frequently-oc-curring formula CAΛBANA XAMBPH, presents for reverse the inscription ΠAMΦIΛOC—TYPANNOC—ΠAPAΔOΞOC —EKATH—EΠHKOW—EYXHN : which seems to mark the gem for an *ex voto*, dedicated by Pamphilus to Hecate in return for some unlooked-for piece of good luck. Another, No. 625, inscribed ΘWX—ΘWXAM—CWZE BAPIN, invokes this oddly-titled Power[4] to protect Baris. In No. 611, five lines of unintelligible letters have for reverse CHC—OMO-NOIAC, showing that the former contained a charm for

---

[3] Rud. E. Raspe, Catalogue raisonné d'une collection générale de pierres gravées, &c., moulées par J. Tassie. In English and French. London, 2 vols.,

[4] " Amidst, amidst them," Heb, per-haps equivalent to " Omnipresent Spirit," or perhaps. " Thou that sittest between the Cherubim."

ensuring concord between the donor and the wearer of the jasper.

It may not be out of place here to observe that certain prescriptions of those eminent Roman physicians, Alexander, Marcellus, and Sammonicus (to be quoted under their proper heading) afford reasonable ground for suspicion, that amongst those legacies of the hidden wisdom of Egypt, the regular, as yet untranslated Gnostic formulæ, many, instead of enjoying the high dignity of being passports to eternal bliss, or else words of power over demons, were to those that understood them, mere charms against the gout and colic—complaints which seem to have provokingly set at defiance the legitimate practice of the sons of Esculapius. For Egypt continued under the Cæsars, a great centre of medical science: Pliny, when mentioning the introduction from that region, the land of lepers, into Italy, of the *mentagra*, face-leprosy, adds that it brought over to Rome a multitude of practitioners, who attended to that disease exclusively. Their mode of treatment was deep cauterization, the remedy being, says the historian, worse than the evil itself, from the frightful disfigurement of the face resulting therefrom. The profits accruing to these empirics were enormous ; they contracted beforehand for a fixed sum, on the terms of "no cure no pay," and arranged their price accordingly. Manilius Cornutus, governor of Aquitaine, is quoted as having paid II.s.cc. (*ducenta* must be meant) or about 200*l.* for the job.

To return to amulets in their strictest sense. One of the most singular, and frequently occurring both on bas-reliefs and gems, represents the dreaded Eye itself as the centre of a circle of symbols radiating from it, and all working together to baffle its stroke. A Praun gem displays the organ of fascination, thus circumscribed by a lion, stag, dog, thunderbolt, dove, and serpent ; the easily recognisable attributes of the deities presiding over the days of the week, whose influence and protection against the *malocchio* were thereby ingeniously invoked. But the completest set of all the amulets most in repute amongst the Romans was that making up the necklace lately found on the skeleton of a Pompeian lady, in the house of Holconius. Separated by beads and canopic vases hang terminal figures of Isis, Anubis, and Silenus, two jackals, two phalli, an open hand, a *manus obscœna*, astragal, wheel, die, bunch of grapes, pine-cone, panther, with a cigala forming the centre. This discovery explains the use of the same objects so often turned up separately.

The *bulla*, a gold case, circular or heart-shaped, worn round the neck by the Roman boys, was a true amulet, for in the beginning, says Macrobius, it was the special ornament · of the victorious general in the triumphal procession, " having enclosed within it such remedies as they esteemed the most efficacious against the stroke of envy." [5] Probably this hidden safeguard was some written spell, for the *bulla* came from the Etruscans, those great charm-mongers of Italy. In fact the specimen (No. 254, Mus. Nap. III.) at Paris was found when opened to contain, folded up, a thin leaf of silver, inscribed with eighteen lines in Greek, mixed with cyphers, interpreted as a prayer to the gods of Olympus, joined with an invocation of the infernal deities. This " Etruscum aurum," restricted to patrician children, was replaced amongst the plebeians by a leather pouch, " nodus tantum et signum de paupere loto," but with contents of equal virtue. And in addition to the bulla, a number of other fantastic objects, of the same character as in the Pompeian necklace just cited, were strung together around babies' necks, as their portraits often show, furnishing amusement by their clinking together, whence the whole appendage got its name of *crepundia*.

To protect oneself against evil influences by wearing *spells*, that is, as the name denotes, mystic words *written* out upon leather or parchment, is a practice going back to immemorial antiquity, perhaps the very first use to which the art of writing was applied. Pericles, in his last illness, showed a friend calling to see him such a thing, that his women had tied round his neck for a last resource when all medicine failed, saying, with a sad smile, it proved him ill indeed to have consented to such folly (Plutarch). Anaxilas, quoted by Athenæus, describes the Athenian fop of those days as wearing the " Ephesian spell " handsomely printed upon parchment strips :—

ἐν σκυταρίοις ῥαπτοισι φέρων
Ἐφέσια γράμματα καλά.

---

⁵ See in the Archæological Journal, vol. vi. p. 112, vol. viii. p. 166, observations by Mr. James Yates on the bulla worn by Roman boys; several examples are there figured.

This most venerable of charms was the words in an unknown language graven upon the zone and feet of the Ephesian Diana, and preserved to us by Hesychius, viz., ΑΣΚΙ ΚΑΤΑΣΚΙ ΑΙΞ ΤΕΤΡΑΞ ΔΑΜΝΑΜΕΝΕΥΣ ΑΙΣΙΟΝ, whereof the traditional interpretation was "Light, darkness, Himself, the sun, truth." These words, according to Plutarch (Sympos.), the Magi used to recite over those *possessed with devils*; and the name ΔΑΜΝΑΜΕΝΕΥΣ is actually found on a Gnostic amulet (De la Turbie) around the type of a mummy enfolded by a serpent, his good genius. As a title of the sun, its appropriateness to a Mithraic gem is sufficiently obvious. Another very ancient example of a spell is that composed by the diviner, Battus, to drive away pestilence, and sung for that purpose by the Milesians, which Clemens Alexandrinus has preserved:—

ΒΕΔΥ ΞΑΜΨ ΧΘΩ ΠΛΗΚΤΡΟΝ ΣΦΙΓΞ
ΚΝΑΞΒΙ ΧΘΥΠΤΗΣ ΦΛΕΓΜΑ ΔΡΟΨ

where he explains the first four words as meaning Air, Sea, Earth, Sun. The Jews, on the restoration of their kingdom, practised the same custom, substituting, however, for these heathenish words certain verses out of the Law, which, being supposed of power to avert all evil and mischief from the wearer (they were bound round the head), received the appellation of *phylacteries*, φυλακτήρια, that is, safeguards. The same belief yet flourishes amongst Mohammedans, especially the African, who employ verses of the Koran with similar confidence in their efficacy. A remarkable illustration of this is offered by certain Oriental mail-shirts, every ring of which is stamped with some holy word, thus converting the whole into an endless tissue of amulets—in every sense, "decus et tutamen in armis." Now-a-days the same spells, *grigris* is their proper title, are sewed profusely over the dress, enclosed in little metal or leather cases.

That the same fashion was equally prevalent under the Lower Empire is apparent from innumerable passages in writers of the time. To cite one of the most curious, Gregory Nazianzen (Or. xl. 18), exclaims, "Your child hath no need for amulets and spells, in company wherewith the Evil One likewise maketh his entrance, robbing God of his glory amongst the lighter-minded ; but give to him (in baptism) the Trinity, that great and glorious mystery." And the Greek epigram-

matists, with whom, as with the wits of Molière's time, physicians were ever held fair game, forget not to bring in the
superstition for their benefit.   Take this example,

Ερμσγενῆ τὸν ἰατρόν ἰδὼν Δίοφαντος ἐν ὑπνοῖς
οὔκετ ʼἀνηγέρθη, καὶ περίαμμα φέρων.

" In slumber sound was Diophantus laid,
When a dire dream Hermogenes portrayed ;
He saw the leech—enough ! he woke no more,
Spite of the guardian amulet he wore."

Pliny (xxviii. 5) quotes, with ill-disguised ridicule, the
singular superstition of his all-powerful and learned friend,
the " king-maker," Mucianus, who used to carry as a preservative against ophthalmia a live fly tied up in linen.[6] Another
noted man of his day, the Consul Q. Serv. Nonianus, wore
for the same purpose, tied about his neck, a paper inscribed
with the Greek letters **P A** ; the virtue whereof perhaps lay
in their expressing the Egyptian name of the Sun.

Most of the Gnostic stones have clearly been intended for
wear as amulets, and not for setting in rings. a purpose for
which their often large dimensions quite unfit them.   This
last peculiarity would lead one to suspect that such stones
were usually carried about in the purse or zone, both for
their special object and also to be readily producible at pleasure, as credentials amongst the faithful, and as means of
introducing one *illuminato* or *ami de la lumière* to another.
To such a custom, derived from the more ancient *tessara*, by
means whereof the general circulated amongst his troops the
word for the day—" It belli tessara signum,"—does St. John
evidently allude in the promise, " To him that overcometh
will I give a white stone, and in the stone a *new Name*
written, which no man knoweth save he that receiveth it."
The word used here, ψῆφος, a *gem*, contains a palpable reference to the *white* calcedony, that regular material for those
talismans, covered with interminable legends, the attempt at
whose interpretation will, after all his pains, convince the
baffled antiquary of the truth of the concluding part of the
" sainted seer's " declaration.   That such things were

---

[6] Which notion may perhaps more
reasonably explain the frequent appearance of the insect in gems than the usual
theory of its reference to Baalzebub,
whose protection is supposed to have
thereby been secured against those blood-
thirsty swarms of whom he was the lord.

intended to be carried about the person, not ostentatiously displayed, is furthermore shown by the old Arabian story-teller's notice how that the Princess Badoura's talisman, "a cornelian engraved with strange figures and letters," was carried by her in a small purse sewed on to her jewelled girdle.

The devices seen on certain talismans, for example, the lion bestriding a corpse, or the captive bound to a pillar surmounted by a gryphon, almost prove that they were made to be given to him "that overcometh," the neophyte who had passed through all the trials preceding initiation ; and their existence may explain Augustine's "image of the demon purchased with bloodshedding" in the Mithraic mysteries. As to the grand seat and authors of the manufacture we are not left in doubt, for Epiphanius, when mentioning that Manes, after his "Mysteries" and "Treasury" wrote likewise an "Astrology," adds, "For these sectaries are so far from eschewing the forbidden art, that the head and front of their boast is the science of *astronomy* ;[7] and moreover the making of *amulets*, that is to say things for wearing round the neck, *periapta*, and incantations, and all such trickery." The use of *periapta* in their proper sense yet survives amongst the German Jews, for, when the sick man is at the last gasp, the attendants bind about his head and arm certain knotted leather thongs.[8] Similarly, a Jew about to be executed thus prepares himself to meet his fate. And in Turkish medical practice a sovereign cure for apoplexy is to encircle the head with a parchment strip painted with the signs of the zodiac.

That all such matters were properly designed to be tied round, or hung from, the person is sufficiently manifest from their generic appellation, *periapta*. This, with their universal use, appears from Spartian's remark when, to place in the strongest light the capricious cruelty of Caracalla, he says that he put to death " et qui remedia quartanis tertianisque

[7] Another and undesigned testimony, this, to the primarily astrological nature of talismanic figures.
[8] These are probably identical with the phylacteries, according to the actual use of objects so designated Tephillim, in the Hebrew ritual, and worn in the synagogue service on the forehead and on the left arm, being attached by long thongs of calf-skin. curiously knotted. These objects consist of small leathern boxes, enclosing four inscribed rolls, and a single roll, respectively. To these boxes the knotted thongs are attached. The fashion of the Tephillim may be seen in Dr. Smith's Dictionary of the Bible, v. Frontlets.

collo suspensa gestarunt."[9] In fact, the only Gnostic stone known to me as retaining its antique setting is one adapted for the purpose. It is a red jasper, oval, engraved with a mummy erect, having its head radiated, type of the soul released and glorified, inscribed **ABPACAZ** ; reverse, the Abraxas god himself and **IAω** below. The stone, nearly an inch long, is mounted in a rudely-made gold frame, having a broad loop soldered on for the cord, after the fashion of the mounted medallions of the Lower Empire.

This unique example rewarded my search amongst the miscellaneous gems of the British Museum, where, at the same time, I recognised many of the finest in the Gnostic Series published by Chifflet more than two centuries ago— another proof of the well-known axiom, that the curiosities of the entire world ultimately gravitate towards London as their centre-point of attraction. In their number, particular attention is due to the immense sard, covered on both sides with a long formula, agreeing word for word with that on the celebrated Hertz garnet, and Chifflet's calcedony ; a repetition that declares the importance of these mystic words, intended either for recitation over a sacrifice, or to accompany the defunct *illuminato* into the grave, for the same beneficial end as the set of prayers prescribed in the "Schema of the Ophites." A third singular relic, belonging to the last phase of the Gnosis, is a large, egg-shaped calcedony, bearing the lion-headed man (perhaps *Ourotal*, the great god of the Aubians, identified by Herodotus with Dionysos), encompassed with a long legend in the latest Pehlevi, or rather Cufic lettering and agreeing perfectly in style with the latest Sassanian stamps.

An appropriate conclusion to this inquiry will be a description of the "Table of Myriogeneses (properly, Moriogeneses)," alluded to in the beginning. That such Tables formed one great repertory for the talisman-makers may be inferred from Ptolemy's observation in his "Carpus," Aph. ix.[1] : "The figures ($\sigma\tauο\iota\chi\grave{ε}\iota a$), in their rise and decline are

---

[9] Probably alluding to the famous Abracadabra, which the first physician of the age, Sammonicus, directs how to write on parchment and wear for the same purpose. De Foe mentions its general use, and the belief in its efficacy during the Great Plague of London.

[1] See the treatises entitled De sculpturis lapidum, and Liber Secretus fili-

orum Israel, printed from MS. Harl. 80, and MS. Arundel, 342, in the Archæologia, vol. xxx. pp. 449, 451; also the extract from "Le Livre Techel des philosophes et des Indois et dit estre des enfans d'Israel," ibid., p 454, from the French *Lapidaire*, printed by Le Roux de Lincy, in his Livre des Legendes.

affected by the heavenly bodies, on which account the
στοιχειοματικοί employ them by observing the entrance of the
planets into them :" where the Arabic translation renders
the Greek name of these professors by " talisman-makers."
And there is another interesting thing about these strange
creations of the ancient astrologers' fancy; they would seem
to have supplied many of the Sigils which the Mediæval
Lapidaria describe as existing on gems, or " Pierres d'Israel,"
but which, for the most part, do not now present themselves
upon any such relics of antiquity. Scaliger (Manilius,
Not. p. 487), has translated the entire Table, describing the
Ascendants in each Sign as they were represented by the
Arabian astrologers, who, in their turn, pretended to be
transcribing the manuals of their ancient Egyptian prede-
cessors in the science. To give here the *degrees* of the first
Ascendant in Aries alone will amply suffice to exhibit the
truly unclassical nature of the representations themselves,
and equally, their close affinity in taste to the Sigils so
highly valued by the mediæval doctors.

Arsiccan, Mars, First Decanus in Aries, gives courage and
impudence to him that is born under the same.   1st Degree.   Man holding in his right hand a pruning-hook, in his
left a cross-bow.   2. Dog-headed Man with right hand
extended, a wand in his left.   3. Man holding out various
ornaments in his right hand, his left placed in his girdle.
4. Man with curly hair; in his right hand a hawk, in his
left a whip.   5. Two men ; one cleaving wood with an axe,
the other holding a sceptre.   6. King, carrying in his right
hand the orb, in his left the sceptre.   7. Man in armour,
holding an arrow.   8. Man with a helmet on his head, in
his right hand a cross-bow.   9. Man bareheaded, in his left
hand a sword.   10. Man spearing a wild boar.

All these types were expressive of analogous predisposi-
tions and natural qualities in the *native*, under each degree.
Taking the hint from this list, Scaliger explains (and very
plausibly) many of those composite figures carrying zodiacal
signs in their hands, and which are commonly accounted as
Gnostic works, to be in reality genuine representations of
these Myriogeneses, and intended to personify the astral
influence of the particular degree upon the infant whose
destiny it governed.

TALISMANS AND AMULETS.

By C. W. KING, M.A.

MEDICINAL AMULETS AND RINGS AND PROPHYLACTICS.

THE physicians of antiquity had the advantage of one powerful auxiliary, the patient's own imagination, now totally excluded from the regular pharmacopœia, and subsisting only in the practice of those old hags in out-of-the-way country places who still cure burns and bruises, and disperse wens and warts according to the mystic lore of old. The agents employed were natural amulets and spells, of which the old Grecian doctor made as liberal use as any " medicine-man " now-a-days amongst the Red Indians. Such remedial means, according to Pindar (Pyth. III. 90), seem to have formed no unimportant part, nay rather, to have held the first place in the resources of the actual god of the healing art when he set up in business for himself after serving his apprenticeship to the Centaur, his predecessor in the same line. The poet describes how thereupon immediately flocked unto him "all people either long afflicted by natural sores, or wounded by the grey steel, or damaged in body by the burning fire or by the nipping frost ; some he treated by means of *soothing spells*, others by suitable potions, some by applying medicines to their injured limbs, others again he set on their legs once more by the use of the knife."

The descendants of Esculapius long continued to follow so respectable a precedent. Hippocrates declares (and evidently without intending a joke) that spells are very useful as adjuncts to medicines, although of little service by themselves. Even the sceptical Pliny, though he indemnifies himself by an occasional sneer at their absurdity, found himself compelled, by the force of public opinion, to ensure the completeness of his work by filling it with a list of the supernatural virtues, not merely of herbs, but of all sorts of objects which operated when merely carried about the person.

Such being the case, it is very conceivable that the medicinal as opposed to the magical virtues of sigils upon gems, of which Camillo, physician to Cæsar Borgia, has left us so copious a list in his "Speculum Lapidum," as constituting a very important element in the education of the Italian doctor of the fifteenth century, were not from first to last the chimeras of dreaming mediæval monks, but were, many of them, received by tradition from the ancient masters in the art. And what confirms this view is the finding the recognition of the value of charms in the cure of disease ever and anon obtruding itself throughout the works of Alexander Trallianus (who flourished under Justinian), although his writings are in other respects highly commended by competent judges for the knowledge they display of the nature of diseases, and their proper mode of treatment. Further on will be found several extracts from his book prescribing, with the utmost minuteness, the proper mode of applying these powerful arcana. It would be interesting to know the exact nature of the rings sold in the days of Aristophanes, nine centuries before Trallianus' date, for protection against the bite of serpents and noxious insects ; but there is reason to suppose, if the authority of the Arab astrologers counts for anything, that they bore the figure of the creature to be repelled by their virtue. This supposition also would account for the frequency of bronze rings of early workmanship engraved with the scorpion, the fly, and even smaller vermin.

Aristophanes (Plut. 883) makes his " honest man " reply to the common informer in these terms of defiance :—

> "I care not for thee since I wear a ring,
> For which I paid one drachma to Eudemus."

To which the other retorts,—

> "But 'tis no charm against th' informer's bite."

Antiphanes again (Athen. III. 123) mentions another sort, exactly answering to the galvanic rings, whose virtues used to be so wonderfully puffed a few years ago as preservatives from all manner of aches and pains, for he introduces his miser, exclaiming,—

> " In a kettle
> Beware lest I see any one boil water :

For I've no ailment : may I ever have none !
But, if perchance a griping pain should wander
Within my stomach or about my navel,
I'll get a ring from Phertatus for a drachma.'

But to a much later stage of ancient society belong those magical rings whose potency was of higher order, dealing not with natural ills, but with the abstract principle of Evil, an idea totally absent from the graceful mythology of primitive Greece. To their consideration a distinct chapter has been devoted in the sequel.

To return to the subject viewed as an auxiliary of the healing art ; the following are amongst the most interesting of the recipes given by Trallianus. Against the *gout* (B. xi.), "Take a strip of thin gold and, after engraving upon it the words MEY.TPEY.MOP.ΦOP.TEYΞ.ZA.ZΩN.ΦIΛOY. XPI.ΓE.ZE.ΩN., wrap it up in the sinews of a crane, put it into a little leather case, and wear it tied to the ankles. Inasmuch as by these *Names* the sun is strengthened and daily renewed, so is this composition restored unto its former power : '*Now, now quickly, quickly, lo! I say the Great Name wherein quiet is confirmed.*' ΓAZ.AZYΦ.ZYΩN. ΘPINΞ.BAYN.XOAK. '*Strengthen this composition as it was at the first; now, now quickly, quickly.*' "—It is evident that these invocations to the sun are given for translations of the two spells in an unknown tongue ; and the giver's express declaration that they contain the *names* of that luminary sufficiently explain the frequent occurrence of TEYΞ[1] and BAINXO upon our talismans.

Another of his prescriptions, good for the gout and all fluxions :—"When the moon is in Aquarius or Pisces, dig up before sunset the sacred herb called *hyoscyamus* with the forefinger and thumb of the left hand without touching its root, and say, 'I speak unto thee, I speak unto thee, O sacred herb ! I call thee that thou come to-morrow into the house of Phileas, that thou mayest stop the fluxion in the feet or hands of such and such a one. But I conjure thee in the great Name IAΩΘ ΣABAΩO, who hath fixed the earth and fastened the sea abounding in flowing waves, who hath dried up Lot's wife and made of her a pillar of salt, receive into thyself the spirit and the forces of thy mother the earth, and

---

[1] It is actually inscribed under Sol in his quadriga on a large hæmatite of my own.

dry up the fluxion in the feet or hands of such and such a one.' Next day take the bone of any dead animal, and before sunrise dig up the root therewith, saying, 'I conjure thee, by the holy names, Iaoth, Sabaoth, Adonai, Elohim.' Then sprinkle a little salt upon the root, saying, 'As this salt shall not increase, so let not the pains of the patient increase.' Then take the small end of the root and tie upon the patient, but hang up the remainder thereof over the fire-place for 360 days."

As a remedy for the *colic* (seemingly a much more fre-quent complaint with the ancients than in our days), he prescribes the wearing of an iron ring, engraved with this figure, which again is a regular Gnostic device, and to be seen conspicuously upon one of the leaden scrolls from the Vigna Marini tombs.[2] The ring itself is to be eight-sided, and on each side to bear two syllables of the formula :—ΦΕΥΓΕ ΦΕΥΓΕ ΙΟΥ ΧΟΛΗ Η ΚΟΡΥΔΑΛΟΣ ΣΕ ΖΗΤΕΙ. "Fly, fly, ho there! Bile, the lark is looking for thee." He adds :—" Of this recipe I have had long experience, and have deemed it unreasonable not to make it known, being as it is of such great virtue as an *antipathic* to the disease. But I recommend you not to communicate such things as this to the vulgar, but only unto the lovers of virtue and those able to keep a secret. Wherefore also, the divine Hippocrates exhorts us, saying, 'These matters being holy you must declare to holy men alone : to the profane it is not lawful.' Observe that the prescribed ring must be made upon the first, or else the seventeenth, day of the moon's age." For the same com-plaint, he also recommends the wearing an intaglio of Her-cules strangling the Lion, cut upon a " Median Stone." Now such engravings in the rudest style of the Lower Empire are frequently to be met with, having, moreover, the initial of the malady they are intended to combat repeated four or six times on the reverse, in the form of a square, or in two rows, so as to leave no doubt upon the object of the amulet. But all that I have seen are in red jasper, whereas Pliny describes the Lapis Medicus, " so called after the Medea of fable," as black with veins of gold. For the *stone* in the bladder, the same high authority recommends you " to get

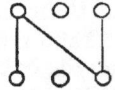

---

[2] Matter, "Excursion gnostique en Italie." Pl. xii.

a piece of copper ore, either Cyprian or Nicanian (as being the purest sorts, one must suppose), that has never felt the fire ; to pick out the veins of metal and beat them up together into the shape of a signet-stone, on which you must engrave a *lion with the sun and moon*, and set the same in a gold ring." This device is often met with engraved on jasper ; perhaps its popularity arose from the general faith in this its particular virtue. And, as regards the special material ordered by Trallianus, I have in my own experience observed disks of a reddish metal set in gold rings, although none bearing the sigil in question. The *colic*, if we may judge from the number of charms against it that have been transmitted from Roman times, must have been a very prevalent complaint amongst the *bon-vivants* of the Empire. Nor is the fact to be wondered at after reading the recipes for the dishes then in most esteem, as given us by the famous Apicius : vegetables uncooked and strong pickles forming so considerable a proportion of their meals, all washed down by oceans of sour much diluted wine. Strange to say, this disease had been unknown in Italy before the reign of Tiberius, and the emperor himself was the first sufferer from the unpleasant novelty. Pliny records how all Rome was puzzled on first reading the word *colum* in the edict put forth by the prince to excuse his non-appearance in the senate. The great frequency of charms against the disorder, an irregular mode of treatment to which we find the most eminent physicians of the day having recourse, is a very convincing evidence that the colic then set at defiance all cure *secundum artem*. Amongst these recipes, the most curious that have come in my way are the amulets recommended by Marcellus Empiricus,[4] an authority well worthy of his surname, such is his fondness for these now unrecognized branches of the materia medica. "Take a thin plate of gold, cut it square, and engrave thereon with a point of the same metal these letters. Roll it up and put it within a tube of gold, stopping up the ends with bits of goat's skin. Then tie the tube with a strip of the same skin upon the right or the left foot, according to which side the pain affects.

L✱M⊙RIA
L✱M⊙RIA
L✱M⊙RIA
L✱M⊙RIA

---

[4] A native of Bordeaux who flourished under Theodosius.

The operation must take place upon the twenty-first day of the moon's age. The wearer must observe strict chastity, neither should he touch a corpse nor enter a tomb."

A second recipe of his for the same malady is to make a ring out of gold thread melted down, engrave on its face a fish or dolphin, and on the shank the verse—

ΘΕΟΣ ΚΕΛΕΥΕΙ ΜΗ ΚΥΕΙΝ ΚΩΛΟΝ ΠΟΝΟΝ.

A good specimen of a ring made according to these directions is preserved in the Galleria, Florence, with, however, a slight variation in the reading :

+ΘΕΟΣ ΚΕΛΕΥΕΙ ΜΗ ΕΧΕΙΝ ΠΟΝΟΥΣ ΚΟΛΟΝ.

A remedy for the *pleurisy*, from which, as he promises, " you will obtain wonderful results," is the wearing of a cerulean Scythian jasper (our sapphirine calcedony) engraved with that common Gnostic sigil[5] s s s upon a bar ; probably a sketchy representation of Æsculapius's staff, (the serpent-twined wand of Egyptian priesthood).

For a *sore throat* you are to write on a bit of paper,

’εἶδον τριμερῆ χρύσεον τοάναδον
κὰι ταρταροῦχον [6] τουσάναδον
σῶζον με σεμνὲ νερτέρων Ὑπέρτατε

Interesting on many accounts is the large Praun hæmatite, now added to the Gnostic series in the British Museum. The type is Mars standing, executed in a very debased style, legend **ΑΡΗΣ ΕΤΕΜΕΝ ΤΟΥ ΗΠΑΤΟΣ ΤΟΝ ΠΟΝΟΝ.** In the field are several unknown letters : in those behind the god's head, Professor Stephens of Copenhagen has discovered the Runes ÆFL(*able*) " Help," which he conjectures to be the *addition* of some Northman, subsequent owner of the amulet. But it is clear to a practised eye that *all* the inscriptions on the stone were cut at the same time, and by the same hand ; and it is easily conceivable that some Goth in the imperial service (they or Franks almost entirely manned the armies of the Lower Empire) had carried with him spells in the mystic language of his ancestral religion, and caused

---

[5] Which invariably accompanies the Chnuphis Agathodæmon on green jasper, which last Galen says was prescribed by King Nechepsos, to be worn as a protection to the chest.

[6] Some epithet has dropped out here, for the iambic is incomplete, probably the missing word may have been ἀργυρέην, for the barbarous names manifestly denote Phœbus and Hecate.

them to be added to the regular formula of the kabalists upon the amulet made to his order. Upon another gem (in my possession) are added characters to the Greek, that have all the appearance of Runes. The high antiquity of this alphabet has been disputed, but on no tenable ground. F. Schlegel has sagaciously adduced one convincing argument in support of the old theory, that the *Scandinavian* Runes were introduced by the ·Phœnician traders, (being indeed their own alphabet slightly modified,) in the fact of their limited number, the actual *sixteen* of the original Punic. Had they been as most antiquaries now hold, nothing more than the Roman letters simplified for the convenience of cutting them upon sticks, they would have equalled the number of their parent. In proof of this comes the Welsh Bardic alphabet, the latest of the Runic, and which possesses no fewer than 43 characters. And again, the genuineness of the Scandinavian is established by repeated occurrence upon the *umbos* found in the Thorsberg moss, Flensburg, found in company with denarii of Severus, and legionary inscriptions.

The *formula* upon the stone last quoted may serve to explain another which, from its frequent appearance, must have been held in high esteem in the same ages of the Empire. It is the figure of a reaper at his work, the reverse inscribed in large characters **CXIⲰN**. The very nature of the subject suggests the reading of the mystic word as a contracted form of σχίσων, "about to cut," whilst from the previous example we may infer that the idea of *cutting* [7] was considered an essential element in the cure of liver complaints, and therefore this sigil of the reaper was esteemed an equally efficacious remedy for that incurable disease. And to conclude, the often cited Marcellus directs any one choking with a bone sticking in his throat to repeat the Homeric,—

μή μοι Γοργείην κεφάλην δεινοῖο πελώρου
'εξ "Αϊδος πέμψειεν ἀγανὴ Περσεφονεῖα

which done would procure him immediate relief.

Old Cato's sure remedy for sprains, which Pliny transcribes for the amusement of his readers, was the utterance of the words HAVT, HAVT, ISTA PISTA VISTA. But the same

---

[7] Perhaps on the same principle by which the belemnite cured the pleurisy, its *pointed* form being analogous to the *piercing* pains of the disease.

historian seriously relates that Julius Cæsar having once had
a dangerous upset in a chariot never afterwards entered one
without repeating thrice a certain spell, *carmine ter repetito,*
(xviii. 4,) which however he very provokingly omits to give
us.

That most famous spell of all, ABRACADABRA, is first mentioned by Serenus Sammonicus, the most learned Roman of
his times, and physician to Caracalla, to whom he dedicated
his poetical Guide to Health, entitled, " De Medicina præ-
cepta saluberrima." This work, remarks Spartian, was the
favourite study of the unfortunate Cæsar, Geta, for attach-
ment to whose cause this true son of Apollo was afterwards
put to death by the imperial fratricide. Severus Alexander,
also, " who had known and loved Serenus," greatly admired
his poetry, putting him on a level with Horace, as Lampridius' expressions seem to intimate. This high authority
orders the word to be written out in the form of an inverted
cone, and declares it of virtue against all disease :—

> " Thou shalt on paper write the spell divine,
> Abracadabra called, in many a line ;
> Each under each in even order place,
> But the last letter in each line efface.
> As by degrees the elements grow few,
> Still take away, but fix the residue,
> Till at the last one letter stands alone
> And the whole dwindles to a tapering cone.
> Tie this about the neck with flaxen string ;
> Mighty the good 'twill to the patient bring.
> Its wondrous potency shall guard his head,
> And drive disease and death far from his bed."

The belief in the virtue of this recipe flourished through
the Middle Ages. It seems alluded to in the Dialogue on
Masonry, ascribed by Leland to Henry VI., for amongst " the
things that Masons conceal" is "the winnynge of the facultye of *Abrac,*" perhaps signifying the possession of this
mystical arrangement of letters ; unless, indeed, one chooses
to suspect in this " facultye " a deeper sense,—some traditionary knowledge of the ancient abraxas religion. Again,
De Foe mentions how people commonly wore the word
written in the manner above prescribed, as a safeguard
against infection during the Great Plague.

As for the etymology of the word, the most satisfactory
yet offered is the compound of the Hebrew *Ha-Brachah*,

" blessing," and *dabberah,* " speak, pronounce," that is, the
Holy Name, or Tetragrammaton, itself the mightiest of
charms.

It is very remarkable, considering its high repute, that no
Gnostic stone bearing such an inscription should be known
to exist. On the other hand, that normal address to Ιαο
ΑΒΛΑΝΑΘΑΝΑΛΒΑ, " Thou art our Father ! " is to be
found on talismanic jaspers arranged in the exact pattern
recommended by Serenus for the paper spell, and probably
so done in compliance with his directions.

TALISMANS AND AMULETS.[1]

By C. W. KING, M.A.

MEDIÆVAL TALISMANS.

CERTAIN Gnostic figures and "Holy Names" continued during the Middle Ages to enjoy as high a reputation as in the classical times. At the very close of the mediæval period, Camillus Leonardi (Camillo di Leonardo), in his "Speculum Lapidum," written in 1502, and dedicated to Cesare Borgia, whose physician he was, when treating upon the virtues of gems and of the sigils cut in them, lays down this fundamental rule :—"Magical and necromantic figures bear no resemblance to the Signs or constellations, and therefore their virtues are only to be discovered by persons versed in those particular arts, viz., Magic and Necromancy ; yet is it most certain that the virtue of the figure may be in some measure discovered from observing the qualities of the stone it is cut upon. And inasmuch as the same stone often possesses different properties, so are figures found made up out of the parts of different animals, expressing the various virtues of the gem itself. This is apparent in a jasper of my own, which represents a figure with the head of a cock, the body of a man clad in armour, a shield in the one hand, a whip in the other, and serpents instead of legs ; all expressive of the several virtues inherent in the jasper, which are, to drive away evil spirits, fevers, and dropsies, to check lust, prevent conception, render the wearer virtuous and beloved, and to stanch the flowing of blood. All such figures are of the greatest virtue and potency." Again, he quotes from Ragiel's "Book of Wings" (a work he styles indispensable to all students of magic) the axiom, "The *Names of God* [2]

---

[1] Continued from Arch. Journ., vol. xxvi. p. 157.

[2] The Rosicrucians made great use of this notion. One of their legends is that Shem and Japhet by repeating six times, as they walked backwards, the great name IABEMIAH, "The God of Increase," restored the virility of Noah, of which he had been deprived by Ham. For they applied the Greek legend of the mutilation of Cœlus by Saturn to the Jewish story of Noah's drunkenness. Again. "The *potent* name NEHMAHMIHAH, coupled with the *delicious* name ELIAEL, puts all the powers of darkness to flight."—Comte de Gabalis.

engraved upon belemnite preserve places against thunderstorms, and likewise give power and victory over one's
enemies." In this doubtless lurks a traditionary reminiscence
of the potency originally attributed to the divine titles in Semi-
tic tongues, that so common decoration of Gnostic talismans,
and also of the sense in which those mystic words were at
that time interpreted. Ragiel cannot be supposed to allude
here to names inscribed in the Latin tongue or character,
seeing that nothing of the sort is ever found upon gems
known to his early period. The Italian Esculapius declares
more than once in the course of his treatise, that all sigils
of potency were the work of the Children of Israel in the
wilderness, whereas those engraved by the old Romans or
the artists of his own times, were merely fancy subjects
(*voluntariæ*), and possessed no other virtue beyond the
natural one of the stone itself. For this reason these *efficacious* gems went by the name of " Pierres des Juifs," or
' Pierres d'Israel," and are often found so denominated in
old inventories of jewels. "Cy après s'ensuyvent plusieurs
pierres entaillées et erlentées lesquelles sont appellées *Pierres
d'Israel*. Selon les saiges philosophes les aucunes sont
artificielles, c'est à dire qu'elles ont etè ouvrées. Premierèment,
en quelque manière de pierre que tu trouveras entaillée á
l'ymage du mouton, ou du lyon, ou du Sagittaire, elles sont
consacrées du signe du ciel. Elles sont très vertueuses car
elles rendent l'homme aimyable et gracieux à tous, elles re-
sistent aux fièvres quotidiennes, quartancs, et autres de froide
nature, &c." (Mandeville's Lapidary, written 1372 ; Archæologia, vol. xxx. p. 454).

In the grand focus of iconoclasm does the most remarkable
example present itself of an adopted relic of heathenism in
the form of the very Kaaba of Mecca. This is a *black*[3] stone,
four feet high by two wide, on which is sculptured a figure of
Venus with the crescent. It is described by Zachder as a
talisman anciently set up to scare away all noxious reptiles.
But the popular notion (which prevailed as early as the
time of Suidas) was, that Abraham begat Ishmael upon this
very stone; or, according to another tradition, tied his camel
to it when he went up into the mountain. The Venus the
Arabs take for the likeness of the hostess of the two angels
Arol and Marol.

---

[3] Probably an aerolite like the Baal of Emesa; the Venus of Paphus, &c.

But the sacred names of the Gnosis in process of time suffered sad degradation ; IAO and SABAOTH themselves became mere spells for making fish come into the net. The mediæval doctors had, long before, read IAO as AIO, and construing this as representing the peacock's cry, promised wonderful effects from a stone engraved with this fowl having a sea-turtle below, and these letters in the field.

The celebrated "Xenexicon" or plague-amulet of Paracelsus, in whose efficacy the learned Gaffarel[4] (librarian to Card. Richelieu) firmly believed, was a paper inscribed with the figures of a serpent and scorpion, to be made when Sol was entering the latter Sign. Another of equal virtue represented a sheep pierced full of holes. But the latest surviving relic of this class of superstitions, is that charm against the plague still believed in by the German boors. The material is a thin silver plate engraved with those holy names of the ancient Kabala thus arranged,—

<table>
<tr><td></td><td colspan="4">+ ELOHIM + ELOHI +</td><td></td></tr>
<tr><td rowspan="4">+ ADONAI +</td><td>4</td><td>14</td><td>15</td><td>1</td><td rowspan="4">+ ZEBAOTH +</td></tr>
<tr><td>9</td><td>7</td><td>6</td><td>12</td></tr>
<tr><td>5</td><td>11</td><td>10</td><td>8</td></tr>
<tr><td>16</td><td>2</td><td>3</td><td>13</td></tr>
<tr><td></td><td colspan="4">+ ROGYEL + IOSEPHIEL +</td><td></td></tr>
</table>

The numerals added together either downwards, across, or from corner to corner, give the same sum, 34 ; though why that particular number should have any special merit must be left for some profound Kabalist (if any yet survive) to explain. This same tablet is seen suspended over the head of "Melancholy" in Albert Durer's wonderful engraving so entitled,—a convincing proof of the importance attached to it in the days of that artist. Its introduction in so conspicuous a place long puzzled me, until I met with the notice of its specific virtue in Justinus Kerner's little treatise "On Amulets."

[4] In his Curiositéz Inouyes. 1632.

The extreme barbarism marking the execution of many
Gnostic talismans would lead one to suspect that their manufacture survived considerably beyond the date usually assigned
for the extinction of the Glyptic Art in Europe. The mere
mechanical processes of this art are so easily acquired, and
the instruments employed therein so simple and inexpensive,
that the only cause for its cessation in any age must have
been the cessation of demand for its productions. But the
Arab astrologers under the Caliphate continue to speak of
talisman-makers and their mode of proceeding as a regular
trade ; the Manichæan branch of Gnosticism flourished far
down into the Middle Age ; the old symbolism was, after
that, taken up and improved upon by the alchemists and
Rosicrucians ; so that such barbarous works, in which every
trace of ancient design is extinct may, with good reason, be
assigned to times long posterior to the fall of the Western
Empire. Of this the most convincing proof that can be
adduced is the so-called seal of St. Servatius,[5] still preserved
in Maestricht Cathedral. It is a jasper, 2 in. in diameter,
set in silver, bearing the rudest intaglio bust of the saint in
the style of a Byzantine medallion ; the reverse, a Gorgon's
head, with a legend plainly a phonetic rendering of the
common exorcism, Μοῖρα μελαινομένη ὡς ὄφις. Again, we
actually find Marbodus, at the end of the eleventh century,
when describing the virtues of the sard, turquoise, and beryl,
directing certain sigils to be cut upon them for the purpose
of enduing the gems with supernatural powers. This he
would hardly have done had gem-engraving been unknown
at the time when he was writing, for at a later period, when
such had really become the case, we observe the mediæval
doctors using the expression, "if a stone be *found* with such
or such a figure upon it ;" thus showing them to be entirely
dependent on chance for their supply of such highly prized
articles, and to have no artists within reach capable of
transferring to gems the potent figures prescribed by Chael,
Ragiel, and Rabanus Maurus. It was not their antiquity
that gave the sole virtue to these gems, for we have abundance of sigils and charms cut in *metal* of ostentatiously
Gothic manufacture. Inasmuch as gems, from their inherent
virtues, were esteemed an infinitely more potent vehicle for
similar arcana than the inoperative metal, the very fact of

---

[5] Figured in the Archaeological Journal, vol. xxi. p. 275.

their not occurring upon gems conclusively proves the in-
capacity of the age for bringing that material into use.
The completest example known of a mediæval talisman is
one figured by Caylus (Rec. d'Antiq. vi. p. 404, pl. 130): a gold
ring, in shape a plain four-sided hoop, weighing 63 grains,
and found in cutting turf a league from Amiens, in 1763.
Each side is occupied by a line of Lombardic letters, in seemingly corrupt Greek, mixed up with easily recognisable
Gnostic titles.

+ OEGVTAA + SAGRA + HOGOGRA + IOTHE +
HENAVEAET

+OCCINOMOC + ON + IKC+HOGOTE + BANGVES +
ALPHA 7IB

+ ANA + EENETON + AIRIE + OIPA + AGLA +
OMEIGA + ADONAI

+ HEIEPNATHOI + GEBAI + GVTGVTTA + IEOTHIN

In most of these spells, the letters GVGVTTA seem to
form an essential part. To give other and full examples of
cognate formulæ :—
The first covers the shank of a silver ring of the four-
teenth century (from Berne), on the face of which is cut the
Ave Maria in disjointed letters : +YRYRRAGVGVBERAL
TERAMIALPLAEZERAE. The second, a silver brooch
(Waterton Coll.) has on the upper side, +EZERA· EZERA·
ERAVERAGAN · +GVGVRALTERANI · ALPHA · ET · ꞷ.
On the flat surface underneath, +AOTVONO OIO MO
OOIO AV. A silver ring (Collegio Romano), reads + MEL
+GEREL+GOT+GVT+HAI+DABIR+HABER+HEBER.
A clue is given with respect to the nature of these interminable formulæ, though not as to their exact meaning, by
our knowledge that the very popular EBERDIABER is nothing more than an aid to memory, each letter being the *initial*
of the word beginning each verse of a prayer, protective
against the plague, written in Latin.[6] But the awful AGLA,
that most potent of all exorcisms, is compounded of the initials of the Hebrew *Atha Gebir Leilam Adonai.* " Thou art
mighty for ever, O Lord !" Mottoes so composed go back very

---

[6] This interesting discovery was made
by Mr. Waterton, in a book on similar
subjects published at Venice in the six-
teenth century.

far : witness, the famous inscription on the banner which gave their name to the Maccabees, *Mi Camohah Bahlim Jehovah.* " Who amongst the gods is like unto Jehovah ! "

Another example (and of more recent date) that tends to illustrate the construction of these mystic forms, composed entirely out of initials, intended for no deeper purpose than to assist the memory in reciting the words of the prescribed charm or prayer, is furnished by the "Cross of St. Benedict," often stamped upon a medal so as to read both vertically and horizontally. The vertical letters stand for " Crux sancta sit mihi lux;" the horizontal for " Ne demon sit mihi dux ;" the letters in the four cantons for " Crux sancti Petri Benedicti." Around runs the legend VRSNSMVSMQLIVB—being the initials in the quatrain,

C. **C** S.
    S
N D S M D
    M
P.   B.
   L.

" Vade retro Satana,
Ne suade mihi vana
Sunt mala quae libas,
Ipse venena bibas."

Lastly, we have an astrological spell, of admirable efficacy, for it is produced by each planet contributing his own initial to make up the mystic **SIMSVM** :

" Post **SIMSVM** sequitur septima Luna subest."

Some Hebrew exorcism is probably expressed in the **BBPPNENA** ordered by *Solomon* to be engraved on a brass or iron ring, to be set with a jasper representing a man's head, and which gave the wearer protection in travel, success at court, &c., &c. **IHS NAZARENVS** was very good against epilepsy, and therefore is still frequently met with on silver rings of later mediæval make ; so was the verse

" Vulnera quinque Dei sunt medicina mei."

But the most notable of all prophylactics for this disease was the letter **T** with the legend **ANAZAPTA . DEI . EMANUEL.** In the Devonshire Cabinet is a cameo converted into an amulet, by the addition of this word, the meaning whereof is as yet shrouded in night, " res alta nocte et caligine mersa." But no charm was of greater force according to the saying,

" Est mala mors capta cum dicitur Ananⱡzapta,
Ananⱡzapta ferit illum qui lædere quærit." [7]

The belief in the virtue of the letter that accompanies the spell, the Egyptian Tau, or " Tau mysticum," goes back to the remotest antiquity. Although undoubtedly originating in the hieroglyphic "Sign of Life," otherwise the "crux ansata," yet the Christian source of name and notion was afforded by Ezekiel (ix. 4) : " Go through the midst of the city, through the midst of Jerusalem, and set a mark (*lit.* "a Tau") upon the foreheads of the men that sigh and that cry for all the abominations that be done in the midst thereof." Where the Vulgate actually reads " Signa eis Tau," perhaps from a tradition of the true meaning of the word. It is a remarkable exemplification of the persistency of ancient beliefs, amidst all the apparent revolutions of religious creeds, that this symbol, after figuring in the Bacchic Mysteries, should have been universally accepted by mediæval faith ‚as the very "Signet of the Living God" mentioned in the Apocalypse. In the painted glass at S. Denys, the Angel was figured stamping the seal upon the forehead of the elect : the legend explaining the subject as SIGNVM TAV. The same mark is the distinctive badge of St. Anthony, an *Egyptian* hermit be it remembered, and in the old Greek paintings is always coloured *blue*.[8]

The phrase " I H S autem transiens per medium illorum ibat," was a safeguard against all dangers in travelling both by sea and land. "And therefore seyen some men when thei dreden them of thefes on any way, or of enemyes, ' Jesus autem, &c.' in tokene and mynde that our Lord passed through oute of the Jewes' crueltie and scaped safely fro hem. So surely mowen men passen the perele of thefes. And than say men 2 vers of the pseaume, 3 sithes, ' Irruat super eos formido et pavor in magnitudine brachii tui, Domine. Fiant immobiles quasi lapis donec pertranseat populus tuus Domine donec pertranseat populus tuus iste quem pos-

---

[7] The complete distich is engraved on a gold ring. found in a tomb at Milan (Waterton Collection). The nearest approximation to a meaning that a very learned Hebraist can elicit from a word is in "The Joy of shapes."

[3] Clarkson states (but without giving his authority—a defect pervading the whole of his learned memoir on the symbolical evidence of the Temple Church), that the T cross was the *mark* received by the Mithraicists upon their foreheads at the time of initiation. He adds that the present Masonic jewel of the G. A. is the same symbol, thrice combined thus,

The three orders of the Egyptian priesthood had for badges respectively the circle, interpreted as signifying the *sun ;* the triangle, *pleasure ;* and the tau, *eternal life.*

ananizapta is the ejaculation: Have mercy upon us O Judge! ' which title moreover was a common synonym for Jehovah with the mediæval Jews.

sedisti.' And thanne may thei passe withouten peine."
(Mandeville, Chap. X.) Edward III. put these same words
for a legend or motto upon his gold noble in memory of his
miraculous escape in the great naval fight off Sluys, an event
also commemorated by the type of the obverse, the king fully
armed standing in a ship. But the same words being likewise
regarded in those times as an alchemical axiom, they were
construed into a testimony to the then current story that
Raymond Lully, the famed possessor of the Philosopher's
Stone, had made (being shut up in the Tower till he com-
plied) the amount of gold required for the new coinage.

Equally popular, too, was the figure of St. Christopher,
and for very good reason, so long as people believed in the
distich—

> "Christophori faciem die quocunque tueris
> Illo nempe die mala morte non morieris."

The· earliest to make its appearance amongst these
spells, and occurring the most frequently of them all, is—

GVTTV . THEBAL . EBAL . ADROS . (VDROS.) MADROS .

in which one is tempted to discover the similarly sounding
Hebrew words, signifying *time, the world, vanity, seek after,
sought,* in the sense of "time flies, the world is vanity, seek
after what is worth seeking for." And this interpretation
is rendered more plausible by what Baccius (De Gemmis)
mentions under " Topazius," that Hadrianus Gulielmus of
Naples possessed one engraved in "antique" Roman letters,
with the maxim to much the same effect "Natura deficit,
Fortuna mutatur, Deus omnia cernit." But inasmuch as
such aphorisms, and couched in that language, have no
precedent amongst existing relics of *ancient* superstitions, I
more than suspect that Baccius' *antique* Roman letters meant
the Lombardic, quite obsolete in his day, when the true
antique alphabet, revived, was alone in use ; and, moreover,
that we have here the true interpretation of the enigma
which has so long puzzled archæologists. Besides the obvious correspondence in the sense, there seems an intentional
agreement in the number of syllables in each legend. Epiphanius (Hæres. xxv.) laughs at the fondness of the Gnostics
for certain Hebrew words, the sound of which had struck
their ear as fraught with deep mystery, although in fact of
utterly trivial import. "Attempting to impose upon the

imagination of the unlearned by the terror of the Names, and the fictitious barbaric sound of the appellations, they give to one of the Powers the title "Caulau cauch," words taken from Isaiah (xviii.), and signifying there nothing more than "hope upon hope." Nevertheless, the sound of **ADROS, VDROS**, irresistibly reminds the ear of the invocation to the Agathodæmon Cunphis in the Hartwell House Collection, **APTOC ΠEINH YΔωP ΔIϞH**, and that some amongst mediæval spells contain fragments of corrupted Greek is a fact that cannot be disputed.[9]

CASPAR or **IASPAR, MELCHIOR, BALTASAR**, the traditional names of the Three Magi, yet more famed as the "Three Kings of Cologne," was an inscription for rings and cups,[1] almost as much in vogue as the words last discussed. The importance so long attached to these names of the "Wise Men out of the East," is evidently connected with some reminiscences of the former Mithraic worship so prevalent throughout the later empire, there being every reason to accept Seel's plausible hypothesis ("Mithra") that under the cloak of Mithraicism early Christianity first grew up and flourished in Gaul and Germany, secure from molestation from the older national creeds. Or again, the same reverence may have had its source at a later period in Manichæism, which was itself only a modification of the Zoroastrian doctrine, for Manes was put to death as a *heretic* by the decree of the œcumenical council of Magi, convoked by Varanes II. to consider the nature of his new teaching. The Magi, therefore, professional brethren of the writer, may well be supposed to have played a very conspicuous part in the "Gospel of Manes," now unfortunately lost. When their names were first published cannot be ascertained ; they do *not* occur where one would naturally expect to find them, in the "Gospel of the Infancy," which gives so particular an account of their visit to Bethlehem. They had been led thither by a prophecy of *Zerdusht*, and received from Mary, in requital for their offerings, the infant's swaddling-clothes, of which present the result is thus narrated.[2] " On

---

[9] For example A**ç**IOS.O.THEOS. A**ç**IOS . ATHA**ℵ**ATOS. (words from the Mass service) often occur, more or less distorted, on rings of this kind. Byzantine influence long continued to tinge the superstition of the Franks. Niquitas (*Nicetas*) of Constantinople and his col-league Udros are named amongst the first apostles of the Albigenses.

[1] As upon the silver rim of a chalice-shaped goblet amongst the Parker plate, Corpus Christi College, Cambridge.

[2] Gospel of the Infancy, ch. iii.

their return their kings and princes came to them, inquiring
what they had seen and done. . . . But they produced the
swaddling-cloth which St. Mary had given to them; on
account whereof they kept a feast, and having, according to
the custom of their country, made a fire, they worshipped it.
And casting the swaddling-cloth into the fire, the fire took it
and kept it. And when the fire was put out, they took forth
the swaddling-cloth unhurt as much as if the fire had not
touched it. Then they began to kiss it, and put it upon
their heads and their eyes, saying,—'This is certainly an
undoubted truth, and it is really surprising that the fire
could not burn it and consume it.' Then they took it and,
with the greatest respect, laid it up amongst their treasures."

The notion that the Three Kings typify the three ancient
divisions of the earth—the first being painted as an European, the second an Asiatic, the third a Negro—seems
borrowed from some ancient representation of the same
regions paying their homage at the "Birth of Mithras," the
Natale Invicti, celebrated on the 25th day of December.
Hence arose the restriction of their number to *three*, although
that of the "wise men" is nowhere specified by either the
canonical or the apocryphal evangelists. Their traditional
names in fact appear from their marked analogy to the attributes of the Solar deity to have been originally no more than
the regular epithets of Mithras himself; Caspar signifying the
White one; Melchior, *King of light;* Baltasar (the Vulgate
form of Belshazzar), the *Lord of treasures.* And the origin
of our festival of Christmas Day is best stated in the words
of S. Chrysostom himself (Hom. xxxi.), "On this day the
birthday of Christ was *lately* fixed at Rome, in order that
whilst the heathens were occupied in their profane cere-
monies the Christians might perform their holy rites undis-
turbed . . . . But they call this day ' The Birthday of the
Invincible One :' who is so invincible as the Lord that over-
threw and vanquished Death ? Or, because they style it the
' Birthday of the Sun.' He is the Sun of Righteousness, of
whom Malachi saith, ' Upon you, fearful ones, the Sun of
Righteousness shall arise with healing in his wings.'"

The very popular spell, already considered, is met with
under many and strangely-distorted forms; being either
corrupted through ignorance, or, what is more probable,
purposely disguised by the insertion of a foreign letter in.

each word. For example, a gold ring lately exhumed in an old castle, co. Limerick, reads,—

+ ADROCS . VDROCS . ADROCS . TEBRAL.
+ TGVSTVS . GVS . TAMGVE.

where, for some mystic reason, the C, thrice inserted, greatly alters the appearance of the familiar charm. Another, in the Collection of the Royal Irish Academy, actually introduces genuine Greek letters, although there is every reason for supposing that the groundwork of the formula remains substantially the same.

+ΠOPOC . SVORCOS . ΠOPCOS . TERRAL.
GVSGYSGVSTRMGVET.

It is much to be regretted that such useful defences of our households should have been allowed to fall into oblivion as were the spells alluded to by Pope in his lines,

"One sings the fair, but songs no longer move,
No rat is rhymed to death, nor maid to love." [3]

Spells contrived especially for the destruction of noxious animals were perhaps amongst the oldest of their kind; Virgil has

"Frigidus in pratis cantando rumpitur anguis."

Justin Martyr likewise [4] mentions, with manifestly the fullest belief in their efficacy, the τελέσματα made by Apollonius Tyaneus against *mice*, and wild beasts; accounting for the fact, by that philosopher's deep knowledge of the secrets of nature. Gaffarel quotes Jonctinus that " Nicolas of Florence, a religious man, made an amulet for driving away gnats under a certain constellation, in certain determinate forms; he made use of the constellation Saturn in a bodily shape, and he thereby drove away the gnats." Something of the kind yet survives in the East : the Persians manage to scare away cockroaches by writing up the name of the cockroach king, Kabikaj, in the places infested by his subjects. In the University Library at Cambridge may be seen a Persian MS. thus defended against their attacks by this venerated name, inscribed thrice upon its cover—how invaluable an ornament to a London kitchen, supposing the title to retain its power over those dusky colonists from the Indies !

---

[3] Dr. Donne's Sat. II.   [4] Quæst. xxiv.

ON A CERAUNIA OF JADE CONVERTED INTO A GNOSTIC TALISMAN.

By C. W. KING, M.A.

FEW relics of antiquity combine in one so many and so widely differing points of interest, with respect to the material, the strangely dissimilar uses to which the same object has been applied in two opposite phases of the history of Man, and, above all, the curious superstitions engendered by its peculiar form, as does the stone brought under the notice of the Institute by General Lefroy at the meeting of February 7th of the present year. The kindness of that gentleman having afforded me full opportunity for the careful examination of this interesting monument, I shall proceed, at the request of some members of our Society, to embody in as succinct a form as their multifarious nature will permit, the observations suggested to me by that examination.

The subject, therefore, of this memoir is a small stone celt of the common pattern, but of very uncommon material (in the *antique* class), being made, not of flint, but of dark-green jade or nephrite, 2 in. by $1\frac{1}{2}$ in. in length and greatest width ; and brought, there is reason to believe, from Egypt many years ago, by Colonel Milner, aide-de-camp to Lord J. Bathurst, during the English occupation of Sicily in 1812. Each of its two faces is occupied by a Gnostic formula, engraved with much neatness, considering the excessive hardness of the material, in the somewhat debased Greek character that was current at Alexandria during the third and fourth centuries of our era.

The most important of these two formulæ has been ingeniously forced to take the outline of a wreath composed of broad leaves, in number *fourteen* (or the sacred *seven* duplicated), and doubtless intended for those of the " Five Trees" that figure so conspicuously in Gnostic symbolism ; the ends being tied together with four broad ribbons. This is a design of which no other example has ever come to my knowledge amongst the innumerable and wondrously varied devices excogitated by the prolific fancy of this religion of mysteries. Upon the four ties are engraved in very minute letters different combinations of the seven Greek vowels, whilst each of the leaves is emblazoned with some " Holy Name," of which many can be easily recognised as constantly recurring in charms of this class ; others are disguised by a novel orthography ; whilst a few, from the uncertain forms of the lettering, defy all attempts at interpretation.

To the first series belong **ABPACA**, " Abraxas," properly an epithet of the sun, but designating here the Supreme Deity ; **IAWOYIE**, " Iao, Jehovah :" **ABΛANA**, " Thou art our Father !" **ΓAMBPIHΛ**, a curious mode of spelling " Gabriel," that testifies to the difficulty ever felt by the Greeks of expressing the sound of our B ; **AKTNONBW**, which contains the Coptic form of Anubis ; **ΔAMNA-MENEYC**, the sun's name in the famous " Ephesian Spell ; " and, most interesting of all, **ΠCANTAPEOC**, who can be no other than the **IΨANTA** of the *Pistis-Sophia*,[1] one of the great Τριδίννάμεις, a Power from whom is enthroned in the planet *Mars*. To the uncertain belong **COYMA**, probably for **COYMAPTA**, a name occurring elsewhere, and perhaps cognate to the Hindoo *Sumitri*, **XWNONIXAP** which may be intended for **XAP-XNOYMIC**, a common epithet of the Agathodæmon Serpent ; **AEIWEHAANHC** ; **NEIXAPOΠΛHC** ; the two last, spells unexplained but very common ; **MONAPXOC** ; whilst **AXAPCIC** and the rest appear here for the first time, if correctly so read.

The other face is covered with an inscription, cut in much larger letters, and in *eight* lines. This number was certainly not the result of chance, but of deep design, for it was mystic in the highest degree, representing—so taught the profoundest doctor of the Gnosis, Marcus—the divine Ogdoad, which was the daughter of the Pythagorean Tetrad, the mother of all creation.[2] The lines 2, 4, 5, consist of Greek

---

[1] Cap. 361. A work ascribed to Valentinus, and the only one of the numerous Gnostic Gospels that has been preserved. It professes to be the esoteric teaching of Christ delivered during the *eleven* years he abode on earth after his resurrection ; and written down by Philip : its system, however. is pure Majianism veiled under scriptural names. But, for that very reason, it throws more light on the actual Gnostic remains as to their types and terminology, than do all the notices of the religion to be found in other authorities collectively. The work was discovered in a Coptic MS. of the British Museum, by Schwartze, and published from his transcript, with a Latin version, by Petermann, in 1853.

[2] St. Hippolytus, Refut. Om. Hæres. vi. 50.

Celt, or Ceraunia, of dark green jade, inscribed with Gnostic formulæ, with an enlarged representation of one of the inscribed faces.

letters used as *numerals*, intermixed with *siglæ*, which, from
their constant occurrence upon monuments of a like nature,
are supposed, with good reason, to be symbols of the planets.
The numerals, on their part, probably denote various deities,
for the Alexandrian Gnosis was the true daughter of Magi-
anism; and in the old theology of Chaldea every god and
astral genius had a *number* of his own, and which often
stands instead of his proper name in dedicatory inscriptions.[3]
Thus, the number of Hoa (Neptune) was 40 ; of Ana (Pluto),
60 ; of Bel (Jupiter), 50 ; of the Sun, 20 ; of the Moon,
30 ; of the Air, 10 ; of Nergal (Mars), 12 ; &c.

A fragment of the *Pistis-Sophia*[4] supplied the "spiritual
man" with a key to the right interpretation of similar steno-
graphy in his own creed. "These be the *Names* which I
will give unto thee, even from the Infinite One downwards. Write the same with a sign (cypher), so that the
sons of God may manifest (understand ?) them out of this
place. This is the name of the Immortal One, AAA ѠѠѠ.[5]
And this is the name of the Voice whereby the Perfect Man
is moved, III. These likewise be the interpretations of the
names of the Mysteries. The first is AAA, and the interpretation thereof is ΦΦΦ. The second, which is MMM, or which is
ѠѠѠ, the interpretation thereof is AAA. The third is
ΨΨΨ, the interpretation thereof is OOO. The fourth is
ΦΦΦ, the interpretation thereof is NNN. The fifth is ΔΔΔ
the interpretation thereof is AAA, the which is above the
throne of AAA. This is the interpretation of the second
AAAA, namely, AAAAAAAA ; the same is the interpretation of the whole Name."

Lines 7, 8, are made up of vowels, variously combined,
and shrouding from profane eyes the *Ineffable Name* ΙΑΩ ;
which, as we are informed by many authorities (the most
ancient and trustworthy being Diodorus Siculus),[6] was the
name of the God of the Jews ; meaning thereby their mode
of writing "Jehovah" in Greek characters.

Line 3 consists of the seven vowels placed in their natural
order. This was the most potent of all the spells in the
Gnostic repertory ; and its importance may justify the ex-

---

[3] On this curious subject see Rawlinson's Ancient Monarchies, iii. p. 466.

[4] Cap. 125.

[5] That is 1000 and 800 tripled. The

next numbers are 10000 tripled, and
so on.

[6] Bibliotheca Historica, i 94.

*Twelve in number, and therefore representing
the Name of God said in the Talmud to consist of twelve letters.*

tensiveness of the following extract from the grand text-book of this theosophy, which sets forth its hidden sense and wondrous efficacy. The primary idea, however, was far from abstruse, if we accept the statement of the writer " On Interpretations" that the Egyptians expressed the name of the Supreme God by the seven vowels thus arranged— **ΙΕΗΩΟΥΑ**.[7] But this single mystery was soon refined upon, and made the basis of other and infinitely deeper mysteries. In an inscription found at Miletus (published by Mont-faucon), the Holy **ΙΕΟΥΑΗΩΑΕΙΟΥΩ** is besought "to pro-tect the city of Miletus and all the inhabitants of the same ;" a plain proof that this interminable combination only ex-pressed the name of some *one* divine being. Again, the *Pistis-Sophia* perpetually brings in **ΙΕΟΥ** invariably accom-panied with the epithet of " the Primal Man," *i. e.*, He after whose image or *type* man was first created. But in the ful-ness of time the semi-Pythagorean, Marcus, had it revealed unto him that the seven heavens in their revelation sounded each one vowel, which, all combined together, formed a single doxology, " the sound whereof being carried down to earth becomes the creator and parent of all things that be on earth."[8]

The Greek language has but one word for *vowel* and *voice*; when, therefore, " the seven thunders uttered their voices," the seven vowels, it is meant, echoed through the vault of heaven, and composed that mystic utterance which the sainted seer was forbidden to reveal unto mortals. "Seal up those things which the seven thunders uttered, and write them not."[9] With the best reason, then, is the formula inscribed on a talisman of the first class, for hear what Valentinus himself delivers touching its potency.[1] " After these things his disciples said again unto him, Rabbi, reveal unto us the mysteries of the Light of thy Father, forasmuch as we have heard thee saying that there is another baptism of smoke, and another baptism of the Spirit of Holy Light, and moreover an unction of the Spirit, all which shall bring our souls into the treasurehouse of Light. Declare therefore unto us the mysteries of these

---

[7] This is in fact a very correct repre-sentation, if we give each vowel its *true* Greek sound, of the Hebrew pronuncia-tion of the word Jehovah.

[8] Hippolytus. vi. 48.
[9] Rev. x. 4.
[1] Pistis-Sophia, cap. 378.

things, so that we also may inherit the kingdom of thy
Father. Jesus said unto them, Do ye seek after these
mysteries? No mystery is more excellent than they; which
shall bring your souls unto the Light of Lights, unto the
place of Truth and Goodness, unto the place of the Holy
of holies, unto the place where is neither male nor female,
neither form in that place but Light, everlasting, not
to be uttered. Nothing therefore is more excellent than
the mysteries which ye seek after, saving only the *mystery of the Seven Vowels and their forty and nine Powers*,
and the numbers thereof. And no name is more excellent
than all these (Vowels),[2] a Name wherein be contained all
Names and all Lights and all Powers. Knowing therefore
this Name, if a man shall have departed out of this body of
Matter, no smoke (of the bottomless pit), neither any darkness, nor Ruler of the Sphere of Fate,[3] nor Angel, nor
Power, shall be able to hold back the soul that knoweth that
Name. But and if, after he shall have departed out of
this world, he shall utter that Name unto the fire, it shall
be quenched, and the darkness shall flee away. And if he
shall utter that Name unto the devils of the Outer Darkness, and to the. Powers thereof, they shall all faint away,
and their flame shall blaze up, so that they shall cry aloud
'Thou art holy, thou art holy, O Holy One of all holies!'
And if he shall utter that Name unto the Takers-away for
condemnation, and their Authorities, and all their Powers,
nay, even unto Barbelo,[4] and the Invisible God, and the
three Triple-powered Gods, so soon as he shall have uttered
that Name in those places, they shall all be shaken and
thrown one upon the other, so that they shall be ready to
melt away and perish, and shall cry aloud, 'O Light of all
lights that art in the Boundless Light! remember us also,
and purify us!'" After such a revelation as this, we need
seek no further for the reason of the frequent occurrence of
this formula upon talismans intended, when they had done
their duty in this world, to accompany their owner into the
tomb, continuing to exert there a protective influence of a
yet higher order than in life.

[2] Evidently alluding to the collocation
of the vowels on our talisman.

[3] The twelve Æons of the Zodiac, the
creators of the human soul, which they
eagerly seek to catch when released from
the body in which they have imprisoned
it.

[4] The divine mother of the Saviour,
and one of the three "Invisible Gods."
Cap. 359.

For the student of the mineralogy of the ancients this celt has very great interest in point of *material*, as being the only specimen of true jade, bearing indisputable marks of either Greek or Roman workmanship, that, so far as my knowledge extends, has ever yet been brought to light. This ancient neglect of the material is truly difficult to explain, if the statement of a very good authority, Corsi, be indeed correct, that the sort showing the deepest green is found in Egypt. The known predilection of the Romans for gems of that colour, would, one should naturally expect, have led them in that case to employ the stone largely in ornamentation, after the constant fashion of the Chinese, and to value it as a harder species of the *Smargadus*. The circumstances under which this relic was brought to England render it more than probable that Egypt was the place where it was found ; a supposition corroborated by the fine quality of the stone exactly agreeing with what Corsi remarks of the Egyptian kind. That *Alexandria* was the place where the inscription was added upon its surface can admit of little question ; the lettering being precisely that seen upon innumerable other monuments which can with certainty be assigned to the same grand focus of Gnosticism. In addition to this, it is very doubtful whether in the third or fourth centuries a lapidary could have been found elsewhere throughout the whole Roman Empire capable of engraving with such skill as the minute characters within the wreath evince, upon a material of this, almost insuperable, obduracy. From the times of the Ptolemies down to the Arab conquest, and even later, Alexandria was the seat of the manufacture of vases in rock crystal. This trade served to keep alive the expiring Glyptic art for the only purpose for which its productions continued to be demanded—the manufacture of talismans, consignments of which must have been regularly shipped, together with the crystal-ware,[5] to Rome, and equally to the other important cities of the empire.

The primitive Egyptians, like the early Chaldeans, used stone in the place of metal for their cutting instruments, and continued its use for making particular articles down into historic times. Herodotus mentions the regular employment of the " Ethiopian stone " sharpened, for a dissect-

---

[5] Dum tibi Niliacus portat crystalla cataplus." Mart. xii. 72.

ing-knife[6] in the process of embalming, and similarly for
pointing the arrows[7] carried by the contingent of the same
nation in the army of Xerxes. The Alexandrian citizen,
half-Jew half-Greek, who had the good fortune to pick up
this primæval implement, doubtless rejoiced in the belief
that he had gotten a "stone of virtue," most potent alike
from substance, figure, and nature, and therefore proceeded
to do his prize due honour by making it the *medium* of his
most accredited spells—nay, more, by inventing a new formula of unusual complication and profundity whereby to
animate its inherent powers. As regards its *substance*, the
stone probably passed then for a *smaragdus* of exceptional
magnitude, and that gem, as Pliny records,[8] was recommended by the magi as the proper material for a talisman
of prodigious efficacy, which, duly engraved, should baffle
witchcraft, give success at court, avert hailstorms, and much
more of like nature. The *smaragdus* of the ancients was
little more than a generic designation for all stones of a
green colour, and the entire Gnostic series strikingly demon-
strates that this hue was deemed a primary requisite in a
talismanic gem—the almost exclusive material of the class
being the green jasper and the plasma.

Again, as regards *figure*, this celt offered in its *triangular*
outline, that most sacred of all emblems, the mystic Delta,
the form that signified maternity, and was the hieroglyph of
the moon. This belief is mentioned by Plutarch,[9] and explains why the triangle so often accompanies the figure of
the sacred baboon, Luna's special attribute, on monuments,
where also it is sometimes displayed elevated upon a column
with that animal standing before it in the attitude of adora-
tion.

Lastly, the supposed *nature* of this gift of Fortune was
not of Earth, inasmuch as it then passed for a holy thing
that "had fallen down from Jupiter," being, in fact, nothing
less than one of that god's own thunderbolts. A notion this
which will doubtless strike the modern mind as so strange,
or rather as so preposterous, that it necessitates my giving
at full length my reasons for making such an assertion.

[6] ii. 86.
[7] vii. 69.
[8] xxxvii. 40.
[9] "De Iside et Osiride," cap. 75. He
adds that the Pythagoreans called the
equilateral triangle "Athene"—a curious
confirmation of the tradition quoted by
Aristotle, that the Attic goddess was one
and the same with the Moon.

And in truth the subject is well worth the trouble of investigation, seeing that the same superstition will be found to extend from an early period of antiquity down into the popular belief of our own times throughout a large extent of Europe.

It is in accordance with this notion that I have designated this celt a "ceraunia" (thunderbolt-stone), and it therefore remains for me to adduce my reasons for giving it what must appear to most people so unaccountable and highly inappropriate an appellation, *Sotacus*, who is quoted elsewhere by Pliny "as one of the most ancient writers on mineralogy," is cited by him[1] "as making two other kinds of the ceraunia, the black and the red, resembling *axe-heads* in shape. Of these, such as be black and round are sacred things ; towns and fleets can be captured by their instrumentality. The latter are called *Bætyli*, whilst the oblong sort are the *Cerauniæ*. Some make out another kind, in mighty request in the practices of the magi, inasmuch as it is only to be found in places that have been struck by lightning." One would have been utterly at a loss to understand what the old Greek had been speaking about in the chapter thus confusedly condensed by the later Roman naturalist, or to discover any resemblance in form between the lightning-flash and an axe-head, had it not been for the popular superstition that has prevailed in Germany from time immemorial to the present day, and of which full particulars are given by Anselmus Boetius in his invaluable repertory of mediæval lore upon all such matters, written at the beginning of the 17th century.[2]

Under the popular names of " Strahl-hammer," " Donner-pfeil," " Donner-keil," " Strahl-pfeil," " Strahl-keil" (lightning-hammer, thunder-arrow or club, lightning-arrow, &c.), and the Italian " Sagitta,"[3] he figures stone celts and hammers of five different, but all common, types ; remarking that so firm was the belief in these things being the "actual arrow of the lightning" (ipsa fulminis sagitta), that should any

[1] xxxvii. 51.
[2] Gem. et Lapid. Hist. ii. cap. 261.
[3] " Saetta" (a vulgar Italian execration). is now restricted to the lightning-missile, the archer's shaft being expressed by the Teutonic "freceia," in accordance with the genius of the language which reserves the old Latin terms for the

things not of this world,—using those of the *lingua militaris* for every-day purposes. The flint arrow-heads found in the *terra marna* of the primæval Umbrian towns, are believed by the peasantry to have this celestial origin, and are highly valued as portable "lightning-conductors."

one attempt to controvert it, he would be taken for a mad-
man. He however confesses with amusing simplicity that
the substance of these thunderbolts is exceedingly like the
common flint used for striking fire with; nay, more, he
boldly declares he should agree with those few *rationalists*
who, on the strength of their resemblance in shape to the
tools in common use, pronounced these objects to be merely
ordinary iron implements that had got *petrified* by long con-
tinuance in the earth, had it not been for the testimony
of the most respectable witnesses as to the fact of their
being discovered in places just seen to be struck with
lightning. Besides quoting some fully detailed instances
from Gesner, he adds that several persons had assured him
of having themselves seen these stones dug up in places
where the lightning had fallen. The natural philosophers of
the day accounted for the creation of such substances in the
atmosphere by supposing the existence of a vapour charged
with sulphureous and metallic particles, which rising above
a certain height became condensed through the extreme heat
of the sun, and assumed a wedgelike form in consequence of
the escape of their moisture, and the gravitation of the
heavier particles towards their lower end! Notwithstanding
this celestial origin, the virtue of the production was not
then esteemed of a proportionally sublime order, extending
no further than to the prevention or the cure of ruptures
in children, if placed upon their cradles; and also to the
procuring of sleep in the case of adults. In our own times
Justinus Kerner mentions[+] the same names for stone celts as
universally popular amongst the German boors; but they
are now chiefly valued for their efficacy in preserving cattle
from the murrain, and consequently the finders can seldom
be induced to part with them.

It must not, however, be supposed that Sotacus picked
up this strange notion from the Teutones of his own age,
whose very existence was probably unknown to him; his
informants were unquestionably those magi cited at the conclusion of Pliny's extract. The Greek mineralogist had
lived "apud Regem," that is, at the court of the King of
Persia, very probably in the capacity of royal physician, like
his countrymen Democedes and Ctesias. In that region

[+] In his little treatise on Amulets.

T

he had ample opportunities of seeing stone celts, for Rawlinson observes[5] that flint axes and other implements, exactly identical with the European in workmanship, are *common* in all the most ancient mounds of Chaldæa, those sites of primæval cities. Such elevations above the dead level of those interminable plains were necessarily the most liable to be lightning-struck ; and hence probably arose the idea that these weird-looking stones (all tradition of whose proper destination had long since died out amongst the iron-using Persians) were the actual fiery bolts which had been seen to bury themselves in the clay. And again, to revert to the German belief, it must be remembered that Thor, the Northern Jupiter, is pictured as armed with a huge hammer in the place of the classical thunderbolt. The type of the god had been conceived in the far-remote ages when the stone-hammer was as yet the most effective and formidable of weapons, and was preserved unchanged out of deference to antiquity, after the true meaning of the attribute was entirely forgotten. Nevertheless, his worshippers, accustomed to behold the hammer in the hand of the god of thunder,—ὑψιβρεμέτης Ζεὺς,—very naturally concluded that these strange objects, of unknown use, found from time to time deep buried in the earth, were the actual missiles that deity had discharged. It is a remarkable proof of the wide diffusion of the same belief, that the late owner of the relic under consideration, habitually spoke of it as a "thunderstone,"—a name he could only have learnt from the Arabs from whom it was procured, seeing that no such notion with respect to *celts* has ever been current in this country. But every one whose memory reaches back forty years or more, may recollect, that wheresoever in England the fossil *Belemnite* is to be found, it was implicitly received by all, except the few pioneers of Geology (a word then almost synonymous with Atheism), as the veritable thunderbolt shot from the clouds, and by that appellation was it universally known. I, for one, can recollect stories, quite as respectably attested as those Boetius quotes concerning the *Cerauniæ*, told respecting the discovery of new fallen belemnites under precisely the same circumstances ; and, in truth, the same author does in the preceding chapter treat at length of the *Belemnites*, and his cuts show that the name

⁵ Ancient Monarchies, i. p. 120.

meant then what it does at present ; but he assigns to the missile an infernal instead of a celestial source, giving the vulgar title for it as " Alp-schoss," (elfin-shot,) which he classically renders into " dart of the Incubus," stating further that it was esteemed (on the good old principle, " similia similibus curantur ") of mighty efficacy to guard the sleeper from the visits of that much dreaded nocturnal demon. The Prussian, Saxon, and Spanish physicians employed it, powdered, as equally efficacious with the *lapis Judaicus*, in the treatment of the calculus. It was also believed a specific for the pleurisy in virtue of its *pointed* figure, which was analogous to the *sharp* pains of that disease, for so taught the universally accepted " Doctrine of Signatures."

The *Cerauniæ* of Sotacus, however, comprised, besides these primitive manufactures of man, other substances, it is hard to say whether meteorites or fossils ; the nature of which remains to be discussed. Photius,[6] after quoting the paragraph, " I beheld the *Bætylus* moving through the air, and sometimes wrapped up in vestments, sometimes carried in the hands of the ministers," proceeds to give a summary of the wondrous tale told by the discoverer of the prodigy— one Eusebius of Emesa. He related how that being seized one night with a sudden and unaccountable desire to visit a very ancient temple of Minerva, situated upon a mountain at some distance from the city, he started off, and arriving at the foot, sat down to rest himself. Suddenly he beheld a globe of fire fall down from heaven, and a monstrous lion standing by the same, but who immediately vanished. Running to pick it up as soon as the fire was extinguished, he found this self-same *Bætylus*. Inquiring of it to what god it belonged, the thing made answer that it came from the Noble One (so was called a figure of a lion standing in the temple at Heliopolis). Eusebius thereupon ran home with his prize, a distance of 210 stadia (26 miles), without once stopping, being quite unable to control the *impetus* of the stone ! He described it as " of whitish colour, a perfect sphere, a span in diameter, but sometimes assuming a purple[7] shade, and also expanding and contracting its dimensions, and having letters painted on it in cinnabar, of which he

---

[6] Bibliotheca, 1063, R.
[7] The Greek purple included every shade from crimson to violet.

gave the interpretation. The stone, likewise, if struck against the wall, returned answers to consultors in a low whistling voice." The grain of truth in this huge heap of lies is obviously enough the fact that Eusebius having had the good fortune to witness the descent of a meteorite, and to get possession of the same, told all these fables about it in order to increase the credit of the oracular stone (which doubtless brought him in many fees) amongst his credulous townsfolk. • Damascius [8] (whose Life of Isidorus Photius is here epitomising) adds, that this philosopher was of opinion that the stone was the abode of a spirit, though not one of the mischievous or unclean sort, nor yet one of a perfectly immaterial nature. He furthermore states that other *bætyli* were known, dedicated to Saturn, Jupiter, and the Sun ; and moreover that Isidorus and himself saw many of such *bætyli* or *bætylia* upon Mount Libanus, near Heliopolis in Syria.

As for the derivation of *bætylus*, the one proposed by the Byzantine Hesychius, who makes it come from *bæte*, the goatskin mantle, wherein Rhea wrapped up the stone she gave old Saturn to swallow, instead of the new-born Jove, cannot be considered much more satisfactory that Bochart's, who, like a sound divine, discovers in it a reminiscence of the stone pillar which Jacob set up at Bethel, and piously endeavours to force Sanconiathon, who speaks of the " living" stones, the *bæthylia*, [9] to confirm his interpretation by correcting his text into "anointed."

But this last *bætylus* is beyond all question the same thing with that described by the Pseudo-Orpheus,[1] under the names of *Siderites*, and the *animated Orites*, " round, black, ponderous, and surrounded with deeply-graven furrows." In the first of these epithets may easily be recognised the *ferruginous* character common to all meteorites (*siderites* being also applied to the loadstone), whilst the second seems to indicate the locality where they most abounded viz., Mount Lebanon.

Sotacus' notice, indeed, of the efficacy of the *bætylus* in procuring success in seafights and sieges, is copiously illustrated by the succeeding verses of the same mystic poet,

---

[8] A stoic philosopher under Justinian.

[9] "Moreover the god Uranus devised *bæthylia*, contriving stones that moved as having life."

[1] Λιθικά, 355.

who, it must be remembered, can claim a very high antiquity, there being sufficient grounds for identifying him with Onomacritus, a contemporary of Pisistratus, in the 6th century before our era. The diviner Helenus, according to him, had received this oracular stone from Apollo, and he describes the rites, with great minuteness, for the guidance of all subsequent possessors of such a treasure, by means of which the Trojan woke up the spirit within the "vocal sphere." This was effected by dint of thrice seven days' fasting and continence, by incantations and sacrifices offered to the stone, and by bathing, clothing, and nursing it like an infant. Through its aid, when at length rendered instinct with life, the traitorous seer declared to the Atridæ the coming downfall of Troy; the stone uttering its responses in a voice resembling the feeble wail of an infant desiring the breast. It is more than probable that Orpheus in describing the Orites, had in view the *Salagrama*, or sacred stone of Vishnu, still employed by the Brahmins in all propitiatory rites, especially in those performed at the death-bed. Sonnerat describes it as "a kind of ammonite, round or oval in shape, black, and very ponderous." The *furrows* covering its surface were traced by Vishnu's own finger; but when found of a violet colour, it is looked upon with horror, as representing a vindictive avatar of the god. The possessor keeps it wrapped up in a linen garment like a child, and often bathes and perfumes it — precisely the rites prescribed by our poet for the due consultation of the oracle of the Siderites.

From all this it may safely be deduced that the "stone of power," whether *bætylus* or *orites*, was in most cases nothing more than a fossil; either a ferruginous nodule, or an echinus filled with iron pyrites. Their being found in abundance in one particular locality, precludes the idea of these at least being meteorites, which latter, besides, never assume any regular form, but look like mere fragments of iron-slag. This explanation is strongly supported by the drawings Boetius gives [2] of what was then called the "Donner-stein," or "Wetter-stein," (thunder, or storm-stone,) and which he very plausibly identifies with Pliny's *Brontias* "that got into the head of the tortoise during thunderstorms," and which is described in another place as the "eye

[2] ii. cap. 264.

of the Indian tortoise" that conferred the gift of prophecy. His carefully drawn figure of this Donner-stein (which also passed for the "gros Kroten-stein," bigger toadstone), shows it to be only a fossil echinus of a more *oblate* form than the common sort. The regular toadstone, plentifully to be seen in mediæval rings, was, on the other hand, the small hollow hemisphere, the fossil tooth of an extinct fish, found in the greensand formation. In that age the Donner-stein was held to possess all the many virtues of the Toadstone, Belemnite, and Ovum Anguinum, in counteracting poison, giving success in all enterprises, procuring sleep, and protection against danger of lightning. But the old physician, so much in advance of his times, cannot help winding up the list of its virtues with the hint, "Fides sæpe veritate major."

SUPPLEMENTARY NOTES ON CELTS AND OTHER IMPLEMENTS USED AS TALISMANS OR VICTORY-STONES.

THE axe-heads and hammer-heads of stone, known to us by the general designation of celts, have, until recent explorations, been regarded as comparatively of rare occurrence amongst ancient relics obtained from Eastern lands and from some other continental countries. Our information, however, in regard to objects of this class has become greatly extended. Mr. James Yates brought before us, in a former volume of this Journal, examples of stone celts from Java ; an interesting specimen obtained at Sardis is figured, vol. xv. p. 178, and some others were found by Mr. Layard at Nineveh. The occurrence of any ornament or inscription upon such objects is very rare, but, amongst numerous stone implements lately obtained in Greece, one is noticed by M. de Mortillet (Matériaux pour l'Histoire primitive de l'Homme, Jan. 1868, p. 9), of which he had received from Athens a drawing and an *estampage ;* it is described as "une hache en pierre serpentineuse, sur une des faces de laquelle on a gravé trois personnages et une inscription en caractères Grecs. L'ancien outil a évidemment été, beaucoup plus tard, quand on a eu complétement oublié son usage primitif, transformé en talisman ou pierre cabalistique."

At the annual meeting of the Antiquaries of the North,

21 March, 1853, under the presidency of the late King of Denmark, several recent acquisitions were exhibited, obtained for his private collection at Frederiksborg. Amongst these there was an axe-head of stone (length about $9\frac{1}{2}$ inches), perforated with a hole for the handle, and remarkable as bearing on one of its sides four Runic characters, that appear to have been cut upon the stone at some period more recent than the original use of the implement. It has been figured in the Memoirs of the Society, 1850-1860, p. 28 ; see also Antiquarisk Tidsskrift, 1852-1854, pp. 258-266. I am indebted to a friend well skilled in Runes and Scandinavian archæology, Dr. Charlton, secretary of the Society of Antiquaries of Newcastle, for the following observations on this interesting relic.

"The first letter is L, and, if we accept the idea that these were Runes of Victory, it may stand for the initial of Loki ; the second is Th, and may stand for Thor ; the third O, for Odin ; the fourth, Belgthor, with a T above it, may refer to Belgthor's friendship and alliance with Thor, and the T stands for Tyr. We may imagine the names of the Northern gods to have been cut on this stone axe to give it victory in battle, just as the old Germans and Saxons cut mystic Runes on their swords, a practice noticed by Haigh in his Conquest of Britain by the Saxons, p. 28, pl. 1, where he has figured amongst various examples of the *Futhorc*, or alphabet of Runic characters, one inlaid on a sword or knife found in the Thames, and now in the British Museum. At p. 51, ibid. pl. iii. fig. 20, he has cited also the Runic inscription on the silver pommel of a sword found at Gilton, Kent, formerly in the collection of the late Mr. Rolfe of Sandwich, and subsequently in the possession of Mr. Joseph Mayer. This relic is now in the precious museum bestowed by his generous encouragement of archæological science on the town of Liverpool. The interpretation given in the latter instance is as follows,—I eke victory to great deeds.[3]

" There was another explanation given of the characters on the Danish stone axe. It was read—LUTHR. O.—Ludr owns, namely, the weapon thus inscribed."

[3] Archæologia, vol. xxxii., p. 321. A spear-head inscribed with Runes is noticed, Journ. Brit. Arch. Ass., vol. xxiii., p. 387. There exist certain massive rings of metal inscribed with Runes, that may have been, as some antiquaries suggest, appended to sword-hilts as charms. One of these rings, lately found at Carlisle, is in possession of Mr. Robert Ferguson, of Morton, near that city

In the ancient Sagas, as remarked in Nilsson's Primitive Inhabitants of Scandinavia (translation by Sir John Lubbock, Bart, p. 214), mention occurs of amulets designated life-stones, victory-stones, &c., which warriors carried about with them in battle to secure victory. A curious relation is cited from one of the Sagas, that King Nidung, when about to engage in conflict, perceived that he had neglected to bring a precious heir-loom, a stone that possessed the virtue of ensuring victory. He offered the hand of his daughter, with a third part of his kingdom, to him who should bring this talisman before the fight commenced ; and, having received it, he won the battle. In another narrative, the daughter of a Scanian warrior steals during his slumbers the stone that was hung on his neck, and gave it to her lover, who thus became the victor. Nilsson observes that stones are found in museums, for instance, a hammer-stone with a loop, that appear to have been worn thus as talismans in war.

It is perhaps scarcely necessary to advert to certain axe-heads of stone, in their general form similar to those with which we are familiar as found in Europe ; upon these implements are engraved rude designs, such as the human visage, &c. These objects, of which an example preserved in a museum at Douai has been much cited, may be "victory-stones" of an ancient and primitive people, but they are now generally recognised as of Carib origin, and not European.

ALBERT WAY.

www.ingramcontent.com/pod-product-compliance
Lightning Source LLC
Chambersburg PA
CBHW022039080426
42733CB00007B/904